LOVE,
VARIOUSLY

— *A Gathering* —

Also by Keith Harrison:

Collections of Poetry
Points in a Journey
Songs from the Drifting House
The Basho Poems
The Complete Basho Poems
A Burning of Applewood (Selected Poems)
Changes (New & Collected Poems 1962-2002)

Translations
Catullus: At the Wedding of Peleus and Thetis
(with Linda Clader)
Sir Gawain and the Green Knight

Radio Play
The Water Man

Non-Fiction
How to Stop Your Papers from Killing You (and Me)

Forthcoming
The Papers of Lady Ann Vaughn
Not Quite Ithaka: Encounters on the Way
When We Come Home (CD)

LOVE,
VARIOUSLY

— *A Gathering* —

KEITH HARRISON

BLACK
WILLOW
PRESS

northfield

© Keith Harrison, 2017
All rights reserved

Except for short excerpts in articles and reviews, permission to re-print any of these poems must be obtained by writing to the author at Black Willow Press

ISBN 978-0-939394-19-7

Cover photo by Keith Harrison
Book design by Mark F. Heiman

for Jenny

FOREWORD

This gathering grew out of a reading given in Canberra last year in which I wanted to make an affirmation, in a dark time, of some of the things that, troubling as they sometimes can be, nevertheless sustain us. A year later, such an affirmation still seems timely.

★

Some of these poems occur in CHANGES: New & Collected Poems 1962–2002 (Black Willow Press), some have been published in various anthologies, including *Best Poems, Australia 2005*, some in literary magazines, including *The Australian Book Review*, and some have not been previously published. My thanks to the relevant editors for permission to re-publish here.

The author gratefully acknowledges the encouragement of Dean Beverley Nagel of Carleton College and the receipt of an Emeritus Faculty Grant in connection with the production of this book. Once again, my warmest gratitude is due to my colleague and friend, Mark Heiman for his patience, generosity and unerring eye.

Canberra, ACT, Australia
& Northfield, Minnesota
2017

CONTENTS

1	Young Bears in an Orchard
2	T-Shirt Poems
3	Three Love Poems from the Japanese
4	A Burning of Applewood
7	I Loved You Once, *after Pushkin*
8	After Buson
9	Before the Blizzard
10	Summer Poem
13	Tomorrow at First Dawn, *after Victor Hugo*
14	A Note from the Interior
15	If at the Edge of Sleep
16	Under the Lime-Tree, *after Walther von der Vogelweide*
18	Dear Chloë, *after Martial*
19	Justice Barrie and Mrs. Barrow
20	A Ball of Tumbleweed
21	A Word in December
22	Falling
23	Man in the Train
24	Spiders
26	Lovers
28	The Ecstasy of Karmstad Karleson
30	Two Women
32	After Heavy Snow
34	Hearing Your Absence Now in Every Room
36	Fourteenth Honeymoon at the Cameron Hotel
38	Revenge
40	Mother and Dad at Ninety-Three
43	Kids
44	Wedding Song
46	Song of the Central Tree
47	Here
48	A Widow of Wild Dog Creek
50	*from* White Wave
53	I Find You Now, *after R.M.Rilke*
54	Creek
56	INDEX OF TITLES
57	INDEX OF FIRST LINES
58	NOTES

YOUNG BEARS IN AN ORCHARD

Just as my hand goes round
    this apple, just so, we took each other
  she having turned toward me
      firmly at dawn, while half asleep.
Later, with a sharp lust
  she bit, breaking the apple —
    the juices flew:
we laughed like honey-bears
  and licked
    in raffish pleasure.
There is no other source than this;
    the hunger
  walks away, there comes
    the gentlest burning.

        here is evening;
    our bodies, the bare stars.
     And once again
    I am hard awake, she having
    turned toward me in
    a flame of moonlit
apple-flesh under
   the black boughs.

T-SHIRT POEMS

Morning flares
in the curtains. Quick
wake up! Take

me now I
will be ravished in
lilac light.

★

Jealousy
has so fine and ear
it can catch

the creak of
bed-springs clear across
five counties.

★

Love occurs
variously. Bears
rub their fur

backwards, till
sparks fly. Then they rromp
and tumble.

THREE LOVE POEMS FROM THE JAPANESE

Thinking of him again,
I dozed off.
but when he climbed
into my bed
I made a mistake:
I opened my eyes.

★

The autumn wind
rasps my body
and I depend on her
as night
depends on night.

★

When I think of her
too much
I put on my bed-clothes
inside out.

A BURNING OF APPLEWOOD

Here we are in our hot boots, the fire
stoked high, all our sins on us and our fur burning.
What a harvest we had of it!
We tramped the fruit-rows summerlong
the smell of mulch thick in our clothes.
So many centuries of mud and apples —
like Ludovico's peasants, feet stogged
in their Sienese earth, flat on the wall
six hundred years. Brilliant planes,
high over, trail white feathers in the sky,
Lebanon withers in flames, out of ecstasy
and murder Islam rises in the desert.
What is this peculiar stuff, water or fire,
floods over us? Did we choose these bitter clocks
that chomp our days?

★

Your fortieth year fell yesterday. I saw you hesitate
there, at the door, then move like a doddard
a half-step, before you turned and smiled, in your eyes
a grey song that your time is winding down,
the apple-trees flecked with obdurate snow, wind
bitching against the pane. We watch
our children growing into their shadows,
silent under a snow-bitten tree, while the dog
drags his hurt paw across the threshhold.

★

The trees are ours but we will never own them.
We cut them back, pluck off the fruit, their liquor
stains our tongues. I do not understand
the language of aphids, black beetles that flash
their rainbow backs in the yellow light. These moments
are given, then something carries them away.

★

Handel was taken with the exactest ways
a theme could change and change and always hold,
and Monet could never quite still the light
that played across his waterlilies
though he paint till time go black again. Today
I watch the light curve down a booming wave,
amazed and maddened by its single repetition
as it spumes always in the wind.

★

I have given up parsing the volatile verbs of love.
Here are our bodies
glistening after bathing, yours ivory
and lithe, mine stocky work-horse that bears me well.
and here's Responsibility, and Money —
a roof that needs repair. Good nouns.

★

The rhetoric crumbles in the end, goes down in the dump
with old paint-cans and busted wardrobes,
kewpie dolls grown obsolete by staying young.
Some afternoons the silence washes over us
like a mallow sunset in a room without music.

We stand in that quiet light and gradually burn.

★

Branches click in the starlight.
There are creatures
snuffing our roots. The brandy glows
and spreads its fumes, the applewood
crackles with a bright malevolence.

I LOVED YOU ONCE

I loved you once: sometimes my love can still
warm its own ashes with a tiny flame;
but be at peace, I would not have you dwell
on that — no cause for sadness or for blame.

I loved you quietly, expecting nothing;
now shy, now jealous, racked by fires of hell.
and yet my love was firm, gentle as breathing —
Pray God another love you half so well.

after Pushkin

AFTER BUSON

I step into our bedroom:
sudden chill.

I have snapped
my dead wife's comb
under my heel.

BEFORE THE BLIZZARD

Great walls of it, seething in, fast, from Mexico,
riding over thruways, filling heads with ice.
I have known you nine days, and many seasons,
but none like this, that's why I came
down a dry road, quickly, the lawns
green in deep December, to fetch you
from your cool sonata.

The house will rock as tall surf
thumps the southern wall;
we'll hunker down, thinking of people on the plain,
wind dragging at their raw-hide roots
and the barn raccoon under the splitting shingles;

and these cats beside us, with sharp eyes,
their clever bodies folding
round a warmth that's held four million years
as we stroke them who, more scared
with many fine imaginings than they
as the snow-flak breaks in the hackberries,
listen and guess, and rub our toes,
just this side of sleeping.

SUMMER POEM
for Dorothy

1

You buried your mother
under the belly of the hill.
You did not ask permission:
carried her there, hacked out a hole
and planted her,
then planted a plum-tree over her.
Each year you light a ring of candles
and sing the songs she cared for.
You sing in joy, standing on
her body, and the song goes down from your toes
and into her bones, the city
of insects and minerals and living things
she is quietly becoming.

2

I woke this morning thinking of her
whom I never saw.
Last night, a hungry deer
dragged at her tree
with his blind teeth, and killed it.
You laughed when you saw the toothcuts:
she would have enjoyed his hunger —
the animal, obeying himself.
You will plant another tree in her:
crab-apple, cherry — they'll bloom,
or the deer will savage them.
Let it be.

3

Our daughters bloom
in the late
sunlight and water splashed
on their quick bodies.
Stripped off our stale clothes
plunged with them
down to the floor of the dark pool
among the mud-slime and the pecking fish
rose up blowing spray
rinsing the shadows from our brains
roved like dolphins through
the blue space of summer,
enjoying hunger
work of our hands and backs
belly of the cow pulsing
against our cheeks,
the house climbing the hill like coral
the white moon striding over us
as we slept with the crickets in the juicy grass.

4

Woke this morning, thinking
beauty is, yes, of body.
A thousand books fell from my mind,
leaving only the pattern on the pinewood ceiling.
Thought of the deer's teeth,
our daughters, their small
breasts budding, their shyness —
and then we walked on the living grass
over your mother's body

Over the bones of many people —
Mothers and sisters and exhausted soldiers —
Over all our brothers sleeping under the hill.

TOMORROW AT FIRST DAWN

Tomorrow at first dawn, when all the fields turn white
I'm setting out, you see, I know you're waiting too;
I'll make my way through the forest, over the height
of hills; I can no longer be so far from you.

And as I go, head down, my gaze fixed, my mind lost
in its own thoughts, not hearing any sound and quite
alone, my back bent over and my two hands crossed
in sadness, day, for me, will then be as the night.

Not seeing the last gold fall through the evening gloom,
nor white sails beating toward Harfleur in the late weather,
when at last I arrive I'll place upon your tomb
a sprig of holly and a bunch of flowering heather.

after Victor Hugo

A NOTE FROM THE INTERIOR

She balances a pot on the hissing stove.
It falls off; beans jump out and swim
across the floor. The dog yaps at them, the children
squeal — and she laughs, her body
pulsing with delight; then sweeps them up,
dices and rinses vegetables, her sloe-eyed
daughters marvelling at her rapid fingers.

Sun lies flat across the water
shooting spokes of light through black branches.
Round midnight, the children breathing evenly,
her body alert as a hunting-cat's,
she will complete that difficult chapter,
her quick prose dancing, light and dangerous,
down the page.   The cut vegetables
smell of earth, and her spirit leaps.
After the years of lean ambition
and cigarettes, she has chosen this.
She studies her daughters, who are grubby,
and necessary, whom she will turn
as she can, toward the light. And chosen
this man who shares her body and her days,
these pines, the ever-changing lake-light.

            But not this happiness
that jumps out of spilt beans, and dog-yaps.

That comes of itself — like lively sentences
that flick their tails, and vanish in the stubble.

IF AT THE EDGE OF SLEEP

I think of you, good farmer,
the cattle steaming, your face aflame with pleasure,
I see your hands go out into the world
and what they touch comes alive.
You bring choke-cherries to the kitchen,
under your fingers the dark jam thickens.
Today, as any day, you've no remorse or shame:
your world is Now. Your world is people —
their bodies, healing and desire.

Two summers ago we stood as one;
the ordinary days flowed around us.
I remember tall mornings.
I remember the nights, loud crickets under the stars.
And once I said, it's right together,
and you (and I half-believed you)
'Yes. Our lives are complex, we are needed.
It will be simple, like this, next time around.'

Well, the time of snow, at least, the time of animals
crammed together in the dark, comes round again.
A skin of ice tightens on the creek, a bad wind
hones the shingles.

Loving and unpossessing, you will remain,
and bite the stone of winter, and relish the world.
To others you give the gift of themselves, and you.
I can sense your warm hands everywhere,
shaping and blessing, and slapping hard, when someone
crosses you.
      Earth-smells, the fume
of wild leeks in the maple-mold,
an open mystery, as of new water rising in the pool.

UNDER THE LIME-TREE

Under the lime-tree near the meadow
my love and I sat down, and there
you might discover where we printed
a light patch in the grass's hair —
near the forest in a dale
tandaradei
there trilled a single nightingale.

As I came walking to the meadow
I found my love there in his leisure,
and when he welcomed me so warmly,
Mother of Heaven, so sharp a pleasure!
did he kiss me? Time and again
tandaradei,
look at my lips, their crimson stain.

Teasingly, quickly, in the meadow
we took our bed in the rich flowers;
a prurient man might shake with laughter
if his steps should follow ours,
and, from the roses, he might say
tandaradei
just here, or here, out bodies lay.

Anyone telling we had been there
so close, and still, would bring us shame!
no one will guess, though — all that happened
was just for ourselves and a tiny bird
tandaradei —
only ourselves and a tiny bird,
who'll never tell what things he heard.

after Walther von der Vogelweide

DEAR CHLOË

I can do very well without your face.
Likewise, without your neck, your hands and arms,
your throat, your breasts, and all your other charms.
In fact, since it's so tedious to list
them one by one by one, it might be best
if I lost all of you without a trace.

after Martial

JUSTICE BARRIE AND MRS. BARROW
Two Telegrams, Paris-Melbourne

Buy gloves
and silk panties.

       Right. Send
       finger-size.

       P.S. Dimensions
       of your bum I know
       precisely.

A BALL OF TUMBLEWEED
for Karen and Peter on their Wedding Day

The ball of tumbleweed that danced on empty air
told him of human things, but most of all
how love is a standing still, and chance, and care.

He drove by a ruined farmhouse: no one there.
He thought of their work, reduced now to a ball
of tumbleweed that danced on the empty air

then he braked hard and almost hit the deer
that sprang back frightened to the chaparral,
and thought of love, and thought of chance and care.

Oh yes, your door will slam; weighted with care,
you'll think — the house un-swept gloom in the hall —
your days are tumbleweed on empty air,

then set to work, and the dark day will clear:
it goes like that, the summer and the fall,
for if love's work, it is also chance and care.

Kind chance on your wedding-day has brought us here
to rejoice with you.
                    May your love grow tall,
not as the tumbleweed in empty air,
but in standing still and flourishing. Take care.

A WORD IN DECEMBER

Think of that disenchantment, that sharp breaking
out of the double darkness that we knew —
Was love the unspoken word, renewed in waking,
the cold flame that we tasted, being two? —

For in that abstract world, the day's confusion,
the clear antinomies of fire and ice
dwindled and blurred: sprang out no quick conclusion,
yet, as I read, these images stayed precise:

your laughter, and your warm hands – your breath, whitely
curling against the frosted pane; the bare
trees we saw in the white park, still as the air —

Some say winter's the death of love. If so,
what in your voice, so strongly and so lightly
touched me just now with a flame that burns like snow.

FALLING

As an awkward kid I prayed beside this bed;
I know each chip and nobble at the head
for sometimes when I knelt here I'd imagine
a wild acanthus or a fruited vine
might shoot from the wood as I stared and said
God bless us all and make us prosper

And now, a ten-year exile slowly returning
I wake once more to the cold downright burning
the same pepperoni, and still the milkman's nag
clops up the hill and whinnies into his bag.

Not quite what I prayed for, not really
what I meant. I curl against your warm body;
the bed's too narrow and your knees sharp:
Move over, love, or I'll continue falling.

MAN IN THE TRAIN

A rope of smoke winds slow
across the wide window.

I watch it break in a fretwork
of trees, dissolve a fence, torque

and thin over the stubble. The sun
flares; eyes narrow in the sudden

wash of light. This is
to meet a person whose life brushes

my life. She detains me
lightly, surely.

I rehearse a phrase, a gesture,
knowing there will be no cure.

And finally I am
afraid of journeys. One is not the same.

Is either well
again, or again ill. An old trouble.

Better to turn back. Write. Forestall
all arrival.

SPIDERS

I stare from my study window into trees.
Considering all things, I watch the first snow spill
white seeds across burnt rubble where the barn
towered over us with its cracked spire
almost half a century until
some feckless pot-head changed
the whole thing into fire.

Considering all things and their seasons,
last night I rose to call you, full of delight:
'Can we dine together, tonight or any night?'
Candles, glasses, I had the whole thing framed
and zoomed. Then stopped. The toad of doubt
filled the room. Everything swung about
half-circle. I think it won't swing back.
I have my reasons.

Your husband hated my bones. Dead
ten years, the slightest thought of him can goad
me backwards into anger. The way he carked *Not so*
or fingered the thin fuzz on his weasel head
when bested in an argument, the dumb
weight of his scholarship that hung
like bags of fool's gold under his eyes.
Casaubon in the desert: a dried-up tarn.
Round him nothing flowed.

He will invite himself, sour ghost.
He'll spread his elbows everywhere. The toast
will turn to wood-chips, the vol-au-vent
spawn spiders who'll multiply and starve
the evening with their hairy eyes.
They'll clog our mouths with silence.

Dead or alive
we carry our spouses everywhere.
They cling to us like varnish to a chair.
For many years, a liminal man, I've loved
you well, the way you moved
round difficult things so lightly, lightly,
and found an elegant thing to do or say
while I – correct and diffident –
admired you, and told no one at all,
not even you.

The blade of prudence has a double edge, è vero?
It can turn round and spike you like an arrow.

And even while our living varnish chips and cracks
the whole thing will remain the same:
a dead man's breath will smother every flame
and you'll hurry away rubbing your palm
across the chilled vinyl of his bucket-seat
and flick awake the radio and drive off fast
while a saxophone blares
across black snowdrifts – all three of us
separate now, disaffection rising
to mingle with the stars.

LOVERS

His Afterthought

Then, turning, she said: *Let's make love
between two fires.* And lit the hissing gas one,
trimmed the paraffin flame; spread rugs.
And I was reading, but she took the light.
my body tensed like a wire. And neither spoke.
Outside, a naked tree held the moon's weight
in a branch fork. Within the clock beat louder.
There was a swelling greenness in the groin
and the blood throbbed like a held bird,
and if I was eager for some mystery when
her silks flowed to the floor — when, with a laugh,
she flung her light things to a chair —
after the sweat of it, that fathomless clutching,
now I am hungry for familiar things,
with the burden of traffic on the solid road,
and her moist hair drowsing over my face... Some day
perhaps I'll ask the meaning of those fires.

Her Rationale

It is by subterfuge we hold, anger, fascinate:
say a left kerchief — or a record borrowed.
We work in the interstices of things
in shadows where men are either gauche or noble.
Sometimes I stop short at the mirror, deploring this —
but what of his marauding, the cocky
vanity? One must keep a grain of pride
against this jocular raping. Une machine à aimer.
No, not that!
                And so: unreason, surprise. Moments
he'll pause today: *Two fires. Don't get it.*
Chuckle, lean back. *You know, women are strange.*
Then, on a whim, he'll call. And I will not say:
There are evenings when I like to choose —
and I choose against this caricature you make me.
Would follow bleak nights, gas-ring suppers, for one.
It must not be said. Hold steady. And keep
from that desert where the last trick has failed.

THE ECSTASY OF KARMSTAD KARLESON

Under roof-trees where bantams listen, like snow-
light gliding everywhere in midnight's morning, his glow
quickens globed lobelias, their black clefts flaring
scarlet with his passing, drops into the clearing
right behind the farmer's eyes, startles him
sharp awake beside his slumbering, grim
dream-companion, forty years. What face to show
as dawnlight thickens to noon gold? Mechanical
thump of hooves, his slow body, and still the appall-
ing light in his head that will not leave him, why,
the new one breathing near, lips wide, scarf awry.

One moment of head-fire that sprang in the *Shopping-Bag*
is eating his bones away: his sleeping slag
flared to a mad resin as her hand idled across
his crocodile skin, watching her toss
a black mane sideways with a rough laugh, slam
her hand on the till as if nothing meant a damn
and he knew, through a haze of tractor-fumes and the dragg
-ing muds of spring, he would dream of her throat
bare and pulsing, as when she stroked his coat
and specially when she whispered: *Come back,
old-timer, you got green oats in your gunny-sack.*

Will mean wife-widowing alive, long
spiral down to maple-mould, mad spider-song:
empty kitchen, bump of boot on hearth-stone,
word scorching in the mouth unsaid, dry crone-
spittle, grackles scratching the day; will mean death
wished for, each hour winding toward evening breath.
He feels him there again, laughing among scuppernong
vines, in well-water singeing face, rinsing,
why, hot limbs: *I am too old for this flensing
fire, leave me be, plain man, I am plainsman;
leave me be, old, in elm-shadow, where I began.*

Whistles a worn-out love-tune as he plunges,
man of clocks, into barn-shadow, arranges
pails, quick, locks bin-rails, feels the raw season
rasp his hands, yelps in joy, while among frozen
images, grandsons hung on walls, his dream-companion
dreams on, hating the stranger, the bright one
who ruins her history. It is no woman changes
her world, but a god doused with grape-light.
                                            He reads
parables in bird-song, cow breath, alfalfa seeds —
his wife beside him night after night reclining
in a hell of wakefulness, his face shining.

TWO WOMEN

'I'm leaving now', and then packed up his bag
and called a friend to drive him far away.
'You must have known there's someone else — why drag
the whole thing on and on? What more to say?'
then the doorway went black and the night reeled
and rode into the house like a smoky sea.
She sat an hour, rock-still, then rose and peeled
an apple, left it there to brown, made tea.
Oh there was nothing evil in his going:
he was correct and just in his demands.
But she could just as well prevent the undoing
of twenty years as kill her trembling hands.
She who had stood by, twenty years beside,
now stared at night, empty and terrified.

But this one had resources: *'I'll prepare
cherry-stone clams on mounds of fettucini.'*
It was his birthday, after all. *Why spare
expense? And candles, Brie, and Boccherini.*
The meal was perfect — even the small kisses
she'd planned between the first and second course.
And then, at nine, the bell. She rose. *This is
the lawyer, dear. I'm filing for divorce.*
He hardly flinched. *Then one more cup,* he said.
Please, I insist you try this marvelous blend.
He thought of strychnine, poured cognac instead.
In curlicues of smoke they wrote their end.
The lawyer gone, the husband turned on his heel
and thanked her for the *really excellent meal.*

AFTER HEAVY SNOW

Two whole days, in white explosions,
stars hurled their frozen fragments down
then, last night, the sky became black wine,
stars hardened and we
lunged outdoors and dug, hour on hour
and found the hulk of a car, engine stuck,
doors ice-welded to its body
like wings of a giant beetle. We banged
and cursed and breathed on it
and, just at midnight, made it
rise and roar.

And all the time, arms swinging,
I thought of you, and the hot snakes
watching from the bracken.

Last night I came to my senses:
love is right now or not at all.
We burn in snowdrift or in stubble,
limbs heavy with life in the slow
urgency of noon or midnight, time
still, but always running and, throats hot,
we filled three flagons and drank them down
and told loud stories round the fire, and laughed,
and climbed the stairs to sleep

Thinking of you — watercolor
haze across the hills, creekwater
singing.

I have known you so few days
and so many days my arithmetic unravels.
Sometimes, especially when water speaks
under ice, our thoughts cross,
or when the big tree shakes itself and
basketsful of new snow tumble down.

I peel my glove away, and rub my hand
in the mystery of snow.
Now, with every restless body
gone from the house, except my own,
with starlight caught in the icicles,
I think of you once more
as they drip their minutes down
in intervals too fast or slow
for me, or the night, or anyone to know.

HEARING YOUR ABSENCE NOW
IN EVERY ROOM

the black mouth of the piano open but un-singing,
impatient with the difficulty of words,
I bang the window-ledge
and startle the grackles in the hackberry tree.
They fly off, carking, to my neighbor's maples.
I laugh, and breakfast by myself in a patch of sun;
then plunge into the day and punch five nails
deep in the cedar plank, and feel them
bite home. I check the level, bounce on the steps.

Everything holds.

Now, in a fume of crushed apples, with your kind of clouds
riding over, I taste the satisfaction of being alone;
these limits, these particulars: a few leaves
balanced on brown grass-tips, the log-pile
ready for the saw, and the brilliant house
drifting on its emerald sea.

What is it that I honor with such good blood
around the heart this morning? Ah, it is something
clean and lively, something in you:

> *Each mortal thing does one thing and the same . . .*
> *Selves — goes itself . . .*
> *For that I came.*

And I rejoice that you stand there in
your separateness, your mind brimming with music:
not the evasion but the transformation of pain.
And I honor all that springs
from what, in our double dark,
we touch together, as we move
down into this new winter, keeping our edges sharp,
honest as wheat, and lucky as the river.

FOURTEENTH HONEYMOON
AT THE CAMERON HOTEL

Climb into the high bed from the oak footstool
beside the black-haired girl-woman
who watches you with wide eyes. This is
your fourteenth honeymoon since your house
cracked, one child on each side howling
soundlessly and beating hands, like people drowning
behind glass. And then the pieces
began to drift apart, like rafts on a gun-metal sea:
the stuff of dreams, except that
the day hung over us, with the smell
of sodden leaves, and a few birds
heat-stunned in a tracery of branches.

Climb up, as if you were your own patriarch
five centuries down in the depths
of another country, another time:
Karelia — the silence after cow-bells.
Your night-cap askew in the twilight, toes
pinched on cold floorboards, your wife's breath
curling up like bear-smoke in the gelid air —
as if you were your own grandfather, carrying
root and branch in you: clowns, and wise men,
singing at appointed times around a fire of bones.

Yes, climb up, and find yourself
mistaken again, for you cannot conjure
your central man, your ancient origin —

only his voluptuary cousin, the one
they whipped from the village constantly
especially in May when pine-resin
hisses under the bark, and across the road
a neon flashing **DINO'S BURGERS**
through a surf of pink snowfall.

Wife, womb, woman,
it's warm in here beside you,
as the world turns its back to the sun; looking
for a garden in this terrible snowlight
where the cars swish by — a kind
of wedding-hymn played on the ceiling:
fighting for wakefulness, fighting to keep
the crack from widening any more.

REVENGE

My father whacked me with a piece of wood:
five flashes of pain across my behind
as he hoisted me by the belt. My shirt
was pocked with mulberry-stains where Ronnie Flood
had pelted me all afternoon. I was almost seven.
I'd waited in a blank room in the house and pissed
my pants as he called me to the shed.
All week I hated him, remembering
his confusion as he tried to find
a length of pine to get it quickly done.

                                        If you count them right,
that's more than thirty years ago. Tonight
I walk beside my father and prop his stick
on a rail as we both go down into the water.
One leg's mostly metal, but in the pool
it floats as he swings up on his back,
recalling the time he barrelled across
the estuary under the screaming of the gulls.

He looks up at the ceiling, smiles
as all the old heaviness drops away.

I walk him round while the weak arm from the stroke
kneads the water like a feeding fish, and I say,
Put your head back, you're doing fine .
The chlorine water slops about his ears
as the big clock on the wall
measures out the seconds, watches us all.

I stand on toe-point as we both slide down
into the darker water. It laps
my chin as I grip his belt and hold my father
weightless on my finger-tips.

MOTHER AND DAD AT NINETY-THREE

My father's
winding down, who once
lifted me

high, to watch
a scruffy ape scratch
his fleas, and

higher for
great music, and more,
much more. Please

forgive me
Dad, I would lift you
in your turn

but the zoo's
are shut, and my arms
fail me. So

I stand still
beside you. You turn:
It's okay

*Son, I know,
I understand.* I feel
him sliding

Away. Then
he starts up: *Listen,
I've designed*

*a plane with
eight wings. It will save
the whole town!*

This with such
passion for a mad
second I

believe him.
Words from a country
in his brain

that's always
Young. Now he falls back
and dreams. He

smiles, he schemes.

★

What to say
of my old mother,
Jess, who can

turn a heel
fast, without looking
and still scan

a mis-hit
backhand? She can hear
owls thinking,

cut whopping
turnips right through, skin
eels, but not

the ones Dad
hunts for every night
in his head.

No darkness
in her century
has held her

Down. Her eyes
sparkle as she knits,
correcting

all errors:
of fact, dates — and our
atrocious

grammar.

KIDS

surge like white water round
our legs and round the kitchen;
they ram slices of apple-pie
between their teeth, leaving
bits all over the plate, then bugger off
to shinny up the plum-tree, giggling
so hard they terrify the magpies.
They dunk bread-bits in their Milo,
sprint through the sprinkler, shouting
hell with you and hell with you.

Inside again, they scrinch their noses up
and belch, twice, while Beethoven
rises to Nirvana. Kids run everywhere
wearing grape-leaves in their hair.

                        Green sap
simmering in their bones, kids
renew us each day with their shrieks
and questions, the way their limp
limbs hang over the bed-cliffs, dopey
with dawnlight as we lift them
up to our hearts, smelling of salt
tidewater flats, and bread-loaves
hot from the oven.

                                    for Nicholas and Zofia

WEDDING SONG
for Katrina and John

Your walking here has made no sound at all.
It had the sureness of a signature,
an exactitude of water-drops, or crystals
glistening in a thunder-egg:
                                these footfalls
down the aisle, this walking which
from now, we shall call Katrina and John
came from its own quietness to this door
which none, beside you, can see, though we gather round
while you pause together on its threshhold.

And now the ghosts come crowding in.

If you listen lightly beyond your breathing
you will catch the skirl of bagpipes, and the thrum
of wooden drums and, now and then, the silver
sound of a kantela rising in a smokey hall.
You will also hear rough seafaring men
breaking bones on an iced beach; there are times
when our cells remember everything: such
a charged thunder of benedictions in the air.
These beings have come to encircle you
and bless, as we, the living bless:
John and Katrina, Katrina and John.

I have flown back from England
to make this wedding song for you
in a time of war, when hope and anger
cross in flares on our horizons,
and we have found that wars have their beginnings
in a place more terrible than the nothing
between the stars and closer than the blood
throbbing behind our eyes.
this is a difficult thought, and true
here, in this chapel on your wedding day.

Because you have chosen this, your day,
and because the ghosts of our mothers and fathers
and the ashes of soldiers are trying to speak
here in this chapel
let us give them our courtesy
so that the quietness that brought you here
as the speech of the guns falls away
can echo again, and again, with theirs.
Your walking here has made no sound at all.
It is as if, by simply walking, you have found the way.

Now everything waits. Here is the door. Go in.

SONG OF THE CENTRAL TREE

I tell you, wood
has always been
my father, and why do you think
the big sky wraps me round.

Woodpecker, woodlouse, raven
these wobbling strings of ants
ridiculously busy,
these lovers touching in my shade
all belong.

Times I can dress myself
in thinnest glass,
tread water all day
or drink
the swiveling light.

All's well with me,
and with my brothers:

I am axle, I am home
and with this excellent hold

I turn the world.

HERE

The day was still as honey in a bowl;
the maple-sap came fast, with winter gone
the cattle stood beside the bright snow-pool
their dung packed down and steaming in the barn.
No help for it — go get your fork and spade
for even those who serve the world with wit
are trundling down into the deep barn-shade
and blocking up their nose, and shoveling it.
You hacked and grunted all day at my side;
and then we heaped it, drove it up and flung
great cartloads on the cornfield, near and wide,
breathing new air rich with earth and dung.
Then stood a little while, single and whole
and the day still as honey in a bowl.

A WIDOW OF WILD DOG CREEK

Five years, and still the ash-trees and the ferns
sound with his voice as I wind alone
down Wild Dog Road, by the giant rock
we picknicked on, whose skin still burns
under the slanting April sun.

Once more, I pause to watch his stallion cross
by the rock-shelf where the creek wobbles
between dark roots and the water swirls.
He climbs the steep bank, snatching grass.
This is the place, among these pebbles,

this is the place where I let him go:
I flung him away as one flings a dice;
in white handfuls I cast him loose
on Wild Dog Creek and watched him flow
toward King Island, and the ice.

For months, an absence like a massive bell
not ringing through a yellow daze;
I hated moonlight, the turning sky,
the bawl of lambs; hated the shrill
cicadas drilling in the haze.

He was my music. I hear his words
in all the wildflowers when they flare
and wither in this lovely valley;
I hear him in the banter of birds,
in silence, and the glass-blue air.

He is so close today that I can smell him.
But the agony has gone, and the farm's
my home again. What could I say
this morning, what could I tell him,
when I held my grandson in my arms,

when he turned his eyes on me and, in a flash,
I saw my husband, heard his laugh
as he gazed on every living thing?
I felt my husband rise from his ash.
We are his joyful epitaph.

from WHITE WAVE

A letter from home, black wind
roaring in my brain
the music of division.
Four a.m. I am hard awake:
I dreamed the age of ice had come
and wolves fed on wolves in the empty town.

The cigarette tastes of death,
its mad point follows my hand in the dark.
In my father's house there are many rocks.
Ten years. Ten million years.
Ice in the maples:
wolves feed on wolves in the empty town.

★

I met a woman in a smoky city.
Ten years.
My life, burning —

From that flame two daughters sprang,
flame in their hair.

They gallop their ponies under the hackberry tree.
Plato said we should stand
against our pleasures and our pain —
but Plato was weird and had no children.
Gallop your ponies, kids, the new life climbing in you,
down through the elm-trees latticed
with shadow and sun.

You cannot know the two snakes dancing in your blood,
one pointing down to lust and hunger
the other wriggling up to heaven
and both will sting you into your womanhood
and I will be your father as I can
as you hurl yourself toward your certain fall
and I will be your father as I can —

old busybody, old fuckwit,
                            I'll be your father.

★

The screech-owl speaks again, and we are night.
The same moon of a year ago
hangs in the swamp-willow.
Its feeble light slides down the wall
where the footballers reach for heaven.

I am alone with all my years.
They flood back now and I forgive them.
I forgive my mother for choosing me, no evil:
I forgive my father for refusing me
the rites, he could not know:
I forgive my children their small disdain,
it is the shadow-side of loving,
and I forgive all those who looked on me
to bind them and
I set you free.

And if you screech again, dark bird, screech for the amazing fire
that crackles in your feathers, that scorches
the quick snake thrashing in your nails —
Screech for the fear of things lit up in the terrible
flame of the sun, the night whose rivers
you ride among,
but screech most of all for the marvellous strangeness
of all creatures exiled under the moon
who hunger to know themselves
and, damaged, do not wince and, desolate,
do not break when the stones
cry out in the midnight wind.

I go through the quiet rooms, remembering.

Have I the courage to accept it all?
The moonlight wanders over the wall.

I am alone, and I am home.

The night is warm, and round.

I FIND YOU NOW

I find you now in everything that lives
and all things are my kinsmen: the tiniest grain
in which you sleep, or when your spirit moves
as a huge thunderhead across the plain.

This is your marvelous game, the yielding powers
you breathe through all that's underneath the skies
to swell in roots, vanish in great tree-towers,
or hang in mist, as when the dead arise.

after R.M.Rilke

CREEK

If water. And a red bird, red stone breathing in the branches, staring down. If water, sliding over veined rock in a pulse of sunlight, over our bodies in the water and bright beads flung skyward from our fingers. If water comes like this, then surely. Bubbles across our bodies, sun-froth, look down at the signings of the years: puckers, strength drawn away, as from horses in their uphill furrows, with darker voicings now, stroll, not skip over stones in the starved creek-bed, further down, waiting for rain. This wearing down also a form of fire. And if it comes as a being it is always a being here among flames in the waratah, banksia cones, twisted sleep of angophora limbs, rub our hands against their skins and agree, if water, then surely to love each other is merely a flowing and a letting go.

INDEX OF TITLES

A Ball of Tumbleweed	20
A Burning of Applewood	4
After Buson	8
After Heavy Snow	32
A Note from the Interior	14
A Widow of Wild Dog Creek	48
A Word in December	21
Before the Blizzard	9
Creek	54
Dear Chloë	18
Falling	22
Fourteenth Honeymoon at the Cameron Hotel	36
Hearing Your Absence Now in Every Room	34
Here	47
I Find You Now	53
I Loved You Once	7
If at the Edge of Sleep	15
Justice Barrie and Mrs. Barrow	19
Kids	43
Lovers	26
Man in the Train	23
Mother and Dad at Ninety-Three	40
Revenge	38
Song of the Central Tree	46
Spiders	24
Summer Poem	10
The Ecstasy of Karmstad Karleson	28
Three Love Poems from the Japanese	3
Tomorrow at First Dawn	13
T-Shirt Poems	2
Two Women	30
Under the Lime-Tree	16
Wedding Song	44
Young Bears in an Orchard	1
from White Wave	50

INDEX OF FIRST LINES

A letter from home, black wind	50
A rope of smoke winds slow	23
As an awkward kid I prayed beside this bed;	22
Buy gloves	19
Climb into the high bed from the oak footstool	36
Five years, and still the ash-trees and the ferns	48
Great walls of it, seething in, fast, from Mexico,	9
Here we are in our hot boots, the fire	4
I can do very well without your face.	18
I find you now in everything that lives	53
I loved you once: sometimes my love can still	7
'I'm leaving now', and then packed up his bag	30
I stare from my study window into trees.	24
I step into our bedroom:	8
I tell you, wood	46
I think of you, good farmer,	15
If water.	54
Just as my hand goes round	1
Morning flares	2
My father's	40
My father whacked me with a piece of wood:	38
She balances a pot on the hissing stove.	14
Surge like white water round	43
The ball of tumbleweed that danced on empty air	20
the black mouth of the piano open but un-singing,	34
The day was still as honey in a bowl;	47
Then, turning, she said: *Let's make love*	26
Thinking of him again,	3
Think of that disenchantment, that sharp breaking	21
Tomorrow at first dawn, when all the fields turn white	13
Two whole days, in white explosions,	32
Under roof-trees where bantams listen, like snow-	28
Under the lime-tree near the meadow	16
You buried your mother	10
Your walking here has made no sound at all.	44

NOTES

Justice Barrie and Mrs. Barrow (p. 17)
Sir Redmond Barrie (1813-1880), one of the most prominent citizens of early Melbourne was, among other things, chief planner of the Melbourne Public Library, and founder (and first Chancellor) of Melbourne University. Although he never married, he had a lifelong relationship with Mrs Louisa Barrow, for whom he built a city house in Brunswick Street, Fitzroy. Mr Barrow bore him four children, all of whom took Barrie's name. The two Paris telegrams they exchanged during his trip to England and Europe – the texts of which I happened upon in and article in the Melbourne *Age* – constitute a lucky example of a 'found' poem, which fitted almost exactly into a syllabic form I'd been working with. Barry's life, and especially in his relationship with Mrs. Barrow seems to me a triumph of integrity over divisions of class, and narrow religious *mores*. In this they were both well in advance of their time.

The Ecstasy Of Karmstad Karleson (p. 26)
This is one of the very few exceptions in my work which needs an interpretive note. In some ancient illustrations Dionysius is depicted covered in grape-leaves, the meaning of which is pretty clear. Like most demonic figures in our psyche his dawn appearance can play havoc, as it does in the life of my fictional midwestern farmer. When I first read this poem to a group of students, one of them asked why an old man would become so infatuated with a young woman behind a super-market check-out counter. I said I didn't have an answer, but assured him that this kind of thing happens more often than we might allow.

Song of the Central Tree (p. 44)
Many cultures have celebrated the tree as a sentient 'axis mundi' – one thinks of The Tree of Man, the Tree of Christ, etc., and figures like the giant in *Sir Gawain and the Green Knight*. There are scores of other examples. A recent book called *The Hidden Life of Trees* by Peter Wohlleben even claims that trees are aware of each other's welfare and form a kind of caring community. It was a delight to discover that book many years after I'd written the poem, and it confirmed my conviction that it should take its place among all the other love-poems.

Born in Melbourne and educated there and in Sydney, Keith Harrison has lived in the United Kingdom, Canada and America. He has taught at London University, York University, Toronto, and as a Visiting Professor of English at Monash University, Melbourne. For three decades he was writer-in-residence at Carleton College, Northfield Minnesota, Professor of English, and Editor-in-chief of *The Carleton Miscellany*. His many publications include a dozen books of poetry and translation, including *Points in A Journey, The Basho Poems, CHANGES (New & Collected Poems, 1962–2002)* and a verse translation of *Sir Gawain and the Green Knight,* initially published by the Folio Society of Great Britain and later included in the World's Classics series of Oxford University Press.

His poems have appeared in magazines and anthologies in Australia, England and America in all of which countries he has received literary awards. Since retirement he has divided his time between Minneapolis and Canberra where he's been working on several books, including a prismatic memoir called *Not Quite Ithaka: A Book of Encounters,* which is scheduled for publication next year.

www.ingramcontent.com/pod-product-compliance
Lightning Source LLC
Chambersburg PA
CBHW060217050426
42446CB00013B/3095